CIRCULAR

ON

KINDER & BLEAKLOW

by

JOHN N. MERRILL

Photographs and maps by John N. Merrill

a J.N.M. Publication.

1990

a J.N.M. PUBLICATION,

J.N.M. PUBLICATIONS,
WINSTER,
MATLOCK,
DERBYSHIRE.
DE4 2DQ
☎ Winster (062988) 454
Fax: Winster (062988) 416

Conceived, edited, typeset, designed, paged, marketed and distributed by John N. Merrill.

© Text and Routes - John N. Merrill 1990.

© Maps and photographs - John N. Merrill 1990.

First Published - July 1990.

ISBN 0 907496 59 8

Meticulous research has been undertaken to ensure that this publication is highly accurate at the time of going to press. The publishers, however, cannot be held responsible for alterations, errors or omissions, but they would welcome notification of such for future editions.

Typeset in - Bookman - bold, italic and plain 9pt and 18pt.

Printed by - Elgar Printing Ltd., Hereford.

Cover Sketch - Ashopton Viaduct from Win Hill by John Creber © J.N.M. PUBLICATIONS 1990.

An all British product.

ABOUT
JOHN N. MERRILL

John combines the characteristics and strength of a mountain climber with the stamina and athletic capabilities of a marathon runner. In this respect he is unique and has to his credit a whole string of remarkable long walks. He is without question the world's leading marathon walker.

Over the last fifteen years he has walked more than 100,000 miles and successfully completed ten walks of a least 1,000 miles or more. His six major walks in Great Britain are -

Hebridean Journey....... 1,003 miles.
Northern Isles Journey......913 miles.
Irish Island Journey ....1,578 miles.
Parkland Journey.......2,043 miles.
Land's End to John o' Groats.....1,608 miles.

and in 1978 he became the first person (permanent Guinness Book of Records entry) to walk the entire coastline of Britain - 6,824 miles in ten months.

In Europe he has walked across Austria - 712 miles - hiked the Tour of Mont Blanc, completed High Level Routes in the Dolomites and Italian Alps, and the GR20 route across Corsica in training! In 1982 he walked across Europe - 2,806 miles in 107 days - crossing seven countries, the Swiss and French Alps and the complete Pyrennean chain - the hardest and longest mountain walk in Europe, with more than 600,000 feet of ascent!

In America he used The Appalachian Trail - 2,200 miles - as a training walk, He has walked from Mexico to Canada via the Pacific Crest Trail in record time - 118 days for 2,700 miles. He has walked most of the Continental Divide Trail and much of New Mexico; his second home. In Canada he has walked the Rideau Trail - Kingston to Ottowa - 220 miles and The Bruce Trail - Tobermory to Niagara Falls - 460 miles.

In 1984 John set off from Virginia Beach on the Atlantic coast, and walked 4,226 miles without a rest day, across the width of America to Santa Cruz and San Francisco on the Pacific coast. His walk is unquestionably his greatest achievement, being, in modern history, the longest, hardest crossing of the U.S.A. in the shortest time - under six months (178 days). The direct distance is 2,800 miles.

Between major walks John is out training in his own area - The Peak District National Park. He has walked all of our National Trails many times - The Cleveland Way thirteen times and The Pennine Way four times in a year! He has been trekking in the Himalayas five times. He created more than a dozen challenge walks which have been used to raise more than £250,000 for charity. From his own walks he has raised over £100,000. He is author of more than one hundred walking guides; most of which he publishes himself, His book sales are in excess of 2 1/2 million, He has created many long distance walks including The Limey Way , The Peakland Way, Dark Peak Challenge walk, and Rivers' Way. He lectures extensively in Britain and America.

CONTENTS

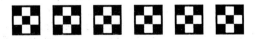

INTRODUCTION

The Dark Peak, named after its dark gritstone rock and peat is an extensive area of moorland occupying the northern end of the Peak District National Park. It is a wild, rugged region famed for its grouse moors. The main two moorland masses are Kinder and Bleaklow with the Longdendale area in the north. Parts of the area lie in Derbyshire, Cheshire, Lancashire and South Yorkshire. In the 1930s it was the scene of mass trespasses by walkers from Sheffield and Manchester, seeking permanent access to the moorland. Today there are agreements making much of the area 'Open Country'. It is the tough walking area of the Peak District and a place not to be taken lightly, even on a clear warm summer's day.

All the walks in this book are based on the **Ordnance Survey Outdoor Leisure Map—the Dark Peak.** Being mostly moorland country the majority of the walks follow recognised rights of way. This book is a guide only and you must take the Dark Peak map with you to find your way. All the walks are circular and from a good car park. Together they take you into diverse scenery, remote places and give you a good insight into this moorland region.

To complete the picture of walks available I have included several of the ma~or challenges of the area. Walks such as the Marsden to Edale and the Derwent Watershed Route are detailed. Both are major undertakings and you should be well versed in map and compass work. I have left the descriptions brief on purpose, for one of the joys of undertaking a walk such as these is the planning of it. Edale is the start of the Pennine Way and 22 miles of it cross our map. My own Peakland Way and Peak District: High Level Route also crosses Kinder and Snake area while the Cal-Der-Went Way crosses the Langsett and Howden Moors to Ladybower Reservoir. My Dark Peak Challenge Walk is also in this area. Combined you have an endless variety of walks to do.

Much of the high moorland areas are now subject to agreement with the Peak Park Planning Board, which has negotiated with the landowners to make this 'Open Country'. This means that by entering 'Open Country' at one of the access points you can then walk where you want. Please observe the Country Code. From the 'Glorious 12th'—August 12th—until December different moors are closed on certain days for grouse shooting. Please do not go on the moors when a shoot is in progress. Details of the days specific moors are closed are posted at the entry points. The moors are closed for only a few days a year, a small price to pay for us to enjoy them the rest of the year.

Being 1,500—2,000 foot high moorland with few footpaths, the Dark Peak is hard walking country. It is a place that demands respect. It is far wiser to retreat than to press on in bad weather unsure of your route. Whilst the main walks in this book are along well used footpaths, you must be able to map read and take compass bearings. You may set off on a fine day but within hours it can change into atrocious conditions, turning a pleasant walk into a nightmare. It is an area to enjoy but enjoy it fully equipped.

 I never tire of walking in the Dark Peak and I hope this book takes you on walks in different sections of the area. I hope also it gives you ideas of other places to explore in the region. you do, have a good walk.

Happy Walking!

John N. Merrill

John N. Merrill

ASHOPTON VIADUCT.

ABOUT THE WALKS

Whilst every care is taken detailing and describing the walks in this book, it should be borne in mind that the countryside changes by the seasons and the work of man. I have described the walks to the best of my ability, detailing what I have found on the walk in the way of stiles and signs. Obviously with the passage of time stiles become broken or replaced by a ladder stile or even a small gate. Signs too have a habit of being broken or pushed over. All the routes follow rights of way and only on rare occasions will you have to overcome obstacles in its path, such as a barbed wire fence or electric fence.

The seasons bring occasional problems whilst out walking which should also be borne in mind. In the height of summer paths become overgrown and you will have to fight your way through in a few places. In low lying areas the fields are often full of crops, and although the pathline goes straight across it may be more practical to walk round the field edge to get to the next stile or gate. In summer the ground is generally dry but in autumn and winter, especially because of our climate, the surface can be decidedly wet and slippery; sometimes even gluttonous mud!

These comments are part of countryside walking which help to make your walk more interesting or briefly frustrating. Standing in a farmyard up to your ankles in mud might not be funny at the time but upon reflection was one of the highlights of the walk!

The mileage for each walk is based on three calculations -

1. pedometer reading.
2. the route map measured on the map.
3. the time I took for the walk.

I believe the figure stated for each walk to be very accurate but we all walk differently and not always in a straight line! The time allowed for each walk is on the generous side and does not include pub stops etc. The figure is based on the fact that on average a person walks 2 1/2 miles an hours but less in hilly terrain.

CHEW RESERVOIR - 12 miles

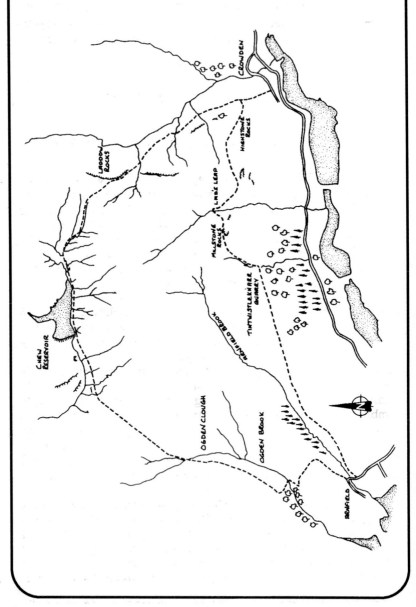

CHEW RESERVOIR - 12 miles - allow 5 hours.

  Crowden—Highstone Rocks—Lad's Leap—Millstone, Rocks— Tintwistleknarr Quarry—Arnfield Brook Arnfield—Ogden Brook—Ogden Clough—Chew Reservoir—Chew Clough—Laddow Rocks—Pennine Way -Crowden.

O.S. 1:25,000 Outdoor Leisure Map—The Dark Peak.

Crowden, just off the A628 road . Grid Ref: SK073994.

ABOUT THE WALK - Starting from the end of the first stage of the Pennine Way from Edale, this walk takes you into an absorbing area of moorland the western edge of the National Park. Crowden and Laddow Rocks are naturally popular but the majority of the walk is through quiet countryside which you will more than likely have all to your self. While crossing the moorland you pass several gritstone outcrops where rock climbing as a pastime developed. You also have panoramic views in all directions.

WALKING INSTRUCTIONS - From Crowden Y.H.A. turn left and walk down the walled lane and cross the Crowden Brook. Go over a stile on the left of a gate few yards later and a few more strides bring you to the Pennine Way. Here, as signposted for Laddow Rocks, turn right and begin ascending. A 1/4 mile later you ascend a ladder stile and reach 'Open Country' beside a small plantation on your right, in memory of the Manchester Rambling Club. Here turn left and begin climbing steeply. Approximately 300 yards later bear left and ascend above a small disused quarry on your right keeping a gritstone wall on your left. The path line is defined and Highstone Rocks are to your left. As you climb you have good views down on to Torside Reservoir behind you and to the tall Holme Moss T.V. mast ahead on your right.

Keep the wall on your left all the time as you curve to your left a start heading due west. A 1/4 mile later the wall turns sharp left; here you leave the wall and turn right and walk along the top of Coombes Clough. The path line is well trodden and stone cairns guide you the head of the clough and a small stream. Cross the stream a contour round the opposite side of the clough along the top of Millstone Rocks.

On your left can be seen the small buttresses of Lad's Leap. Maintain your height past Millstone Rocks for another 300 yards before turning left and following the path on the left-hand side of Black Gutter. A little after 1/4 mile you reach two ladder stiles at the entrance to 'Open Country.' Use the right-hand one and turn right and keep the fence on your immediate left as you walk along top of Tintwistleknarr Quarry. The path is well used and often rather boggy. A 1/2 mile later the path crosses moorland as you begin descending down to the southern side of Arnfield Clough. In the bottom can be seen Arnfield Brook and further down the clough the path becomes a grass track. Continue down the track to the road just south of Arnfield.

Turn right at the road and cross the bridge over the brook. A few yards later turn right and ascend a walled track. Just after entering 'Open Country' the track divides and here you turn left and after 1/4 mile descend to Ogden Brook. Cross the brook and ascend and at the top of the initial slope turn right at the signpost—'Footpath to Chew Valley'. The path is faint at first but the further you climb up Ogden Clough the more noticeable it becomes. After two-thirds of a mile you cross a footbridge and begin ascending over Ormes Moor to the top of Chew Valley. The path becomes indistinct but cairns and later wooden posts help to guide you across this black area aptly named on the map—Wilderness.

Continue to the edge of the valley where you will find a wide footpath. The effort to get here is well worth it for the view down the valley is impressive. Turn right and follow the path to Chew Reservoir which you can see about 1/2 mile away. On reaching the reservoir wall bear right and walk beside the reservoir along the track on its right-hand side. The path from here all the way back to Crowden is well used. Just past the end of the reservoir the path uses a footbridge and at a large stone cairn you bear right, walking along the base of the shallow Chew Clough. Soon you cross your highest point of the day, 1,717 ft., on Laddow Moss before descending to your right. On the moorland grouse can be seen and heard and often during the summer, ring ouzel, curlew and skylarks are spotted.

The path brings you to the edge of the clough with Laddow Rocks on your left. The rocks are a popular climbing ground and one route, known as the Long Climb, is the longest gritstone climb in the Peak District at 105 ft. Descend the wide path and walk along the Pennine Way, heading southwards. A little over a mile later you rejoin your starting out path which you retrace back to Crowden. Alas the walk ends but for me this walk remains one of the most enjoyable outings in this area of the Dark Peak.

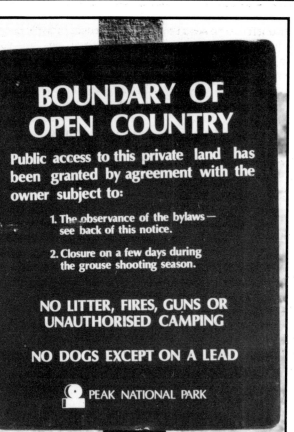

OPEN COUNTRY SIGN.

CLIMBING ON LADDOW ROCKS.

CROWDEN AND BLACK HILL - 10 miles

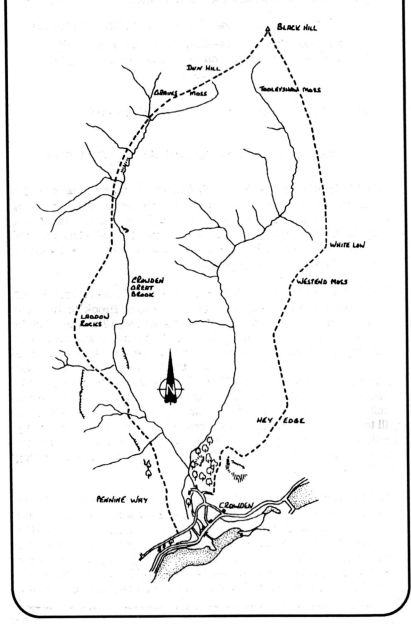

CROWDEN AND BLACK HILL
- 10 miles
- allow 4 hours.

Crowden—Pennine Way—Laddow Rocks—Crowden Great Brook—Grains Moss—Dun Hill—Black Hill I, 908ft.— Tooleyshaw Moss—White Low—Westend Moss—- Hey Edge —Crowden.

O.S. 1:25,000 Outdoor Leisure Map—The Dark Peak.

Crowden, just off the A628 road. Grid Ref: SK073994.

ABOUT THE WALK - The walk follows a 5 mile segment of the second stage of the Pennine Way, from Crowden to the summit of Black Hill. The hill can be atrocious in bad weather and is often a quagmire of black oozing peat. So select your day well ! Despite this it is a very pleasant moorland circuit and one that I have been walking and writing about for several years.

WALKING INSTRUCTIONS - From Crowden Y.H.A. turn left and walk down the walled lane and cross Crowden Brook to the gate beyond. A short distance further at the footpath sign 'Pennine Way via Laddow Rocks' turn right. The path is well trodden as it weaves its way gradually upwards into 'Open Country'. Almost two miles from Crowden the path ascends along the top of Laddow Rocks, a popular gritstone rock climbing area. Beyond the path descends to the left-hand side of Crowden Great Brook which you walk close to for about a mile. The final mile is gentle climbing across Grains Moss and Dun Hill to Black Hill. Whilst you will already have had to negotiate many sections of wet boggy peat, this section to Black Hill summit is almost masochistic. You have to constantly wander from side to side finding the 'driest' possible route.

Black Hill is very aptly named, being all black peat. The triangulation pillar stands at 1,908 ft. upon about the most solid piece of ground around. For these five miles from Crowden you have been following the Pennine Way. Here in the summer long distance walkers bound for Kirk Yetholm in Scotland, some 230 miles away, turn left and begin crossing more boggy ground over Wessenden Head Moor. Here you turn sharp right and head almost due south across Tooleyshaw Moss.

All the time you were walking to Black Hill the tall mast of Holme Moss will have been piercing the skyline . Now you head for the reservoir-filled Longdendale. The path is well travelled as you descend across Tooleyshaw Moor and on to White Low. Although a well defined footpath- it is always wise to carry a compass for in low cloud or mist you could soon lose your way. After White Low you ascend gently to Westend Moss. From here you begin descending more sharply as you cross Hey Moss to Hey Edge. On your right is the steep sided Crowden Little Brook. At Hey Edge you bear right for Crowden a mile away. The path zig-zags its way down between two disused quarries. Down at the road Crowden Y.H.A. is on your left.

❉ ❉ ❉ ❉ ❉ ❉

DOCTORS GATE - REMAINS OF ROMAN ROAD.

CROWDEN YOUTH HOSTEL.

OLD GLOSSOP.

OLD GLOSSOP AND TORSIDE - 13 miles

OLD GLOSSOP AND TORSIDE - 13 miles - allow 5 hours.

Old Glossop—Shelf Brook—Doctor's Gate—Alport Low —Bleaklow Head—Pennine Way—Torside Castle— Clough Edge—Torside Reservoir—Rhodeswood Reservoir —Deepclough—Padfield— Little Padfield—Swineshead Reservoir—Old Glossop.

 O.S. 1:25,000 Outdoor Leisure Map—The Dark Peak.

No official car park but roadside parking at Old Glossop. Grid Ref: SK043948.

Shorter walk—9 miles: *Starts and ends from Old Glossop but instead of going over Bleaklow Head the route leaves Shelf Brook and Roes near Shittern Clough, across Harrop Moss to Torside Castle. Here it rejoins the main route.*

ABOUT THE WALK - Old Glossop is a delightful cluster of 18th century houses and a market cross. It makes an apt starting point for exploring the western side of Bleaklow. The circuit crosses high moorland and follows part of the Pennine Way. To return to Old Glossop we walk close to four reservoirs and past further 18th century buildings. The principal route is a long walk but can be shortened to 9 miles by a direct crossing of Harrop Moor. This is a good route in poor conditions but does require the accurate use of map and compass.

WALKING INSTRUCTIONS - From The Queens Inn in Old Glossop walk up Shepley Street Past the factory buildings of Glossop Superalloys, Ltd. Keep Shelf Brook on your right. You walk along a wide track and about 3/4 mile (15 minutes) from the inn you see a fenced path leading off to your left to 'Open Country.' This is the path you take for the shorter walk. On the longer walk continue on the track and a further 1/4 mile brings you to 'Open Country.' Carry straight ahead beginning ascend and following the line of a Roman road which linked the fort of Melandra near Glossop with Navio, the fort at Brough in the Hope Valley. At first you walk close to Shelf Brook but after 1/2 mile you leave its banks and a mile later reach

17

the summit of the 'road'. Here there is a large cairn and the Pennine Way crosses diagonally.

Turn left and follow the well-travelled Pennine Way over Alport Low and then on to peat moorland to Bleaklow Head, two miles from Doctor's Gate. The name Doctor's Gate is reputed to derive from a local Dr. Faust who had a horse race with the Devil, a won ! The Devil was so annoyed at losing that he scratched with I finger a long gash in the moorland. Marked on some maps this known as Devil's Dike. The crossing at Bleaklow Head, 2,060ft. can be very bleak in bad weather and a compass and ability to use one is very necessary. In good weather there is no problem and time permits a visit to Higher Shelf Stones to the west of the Pennine Way is recommended to see one of the many aircraft wrecks in the Dark Peak. Here are the remains of a Superfortress B-29 (the type which dropped the atomic bomb on Hiroshima) which crashed November 3rd, 1948.

From Bleaklow Head keep on the Pennine Way as it curves north-westwards down Wildboar Grain and past the large mound Torside Castle, which the shorter route passes. The wide path keeps to the edge of Torside Clough before going to the left of Reaps Farm. After a ladder stile descend to the road and turn left, still on the Pennine Way. At the B6105 road turn right and cross the rail crossing beside Torside signal box. Turn left immediately afterwards down the Water Board road. Upon reaching the dam wall Torside Reservoir, ascend the ladder stile on your left and follow the grass track across the fields. This is delightful walking and great contrast from the moor-land section. In almost a mile you reach the track over the dam wall of Rhodeswood Reservoir. He turn left to the 18th century houses of Deepclough—the barn dated 1771.

Continue past the houses and, where the road forks, keep on the main road which curves round to your left. Just after crossing the railway line opposite Vale House signal box, turn right through the stile and follow the signposted path—Padfield, 3/4 mile. The path keeps close to the railway line at first but after three fields swings away from it and becomes a walled lane to Padfield. You reach the road in Padfield opposite Rowan Cottage. Turn left and 50 yards later turn right along Peel Street, which goes to one house. At the end of this short 'No Through Road' the stile is in the left-hand corner. Cross the field beyond bearing left to walk to the road; Little Padfield, which again has beautiful 18th century houses. The stiles bring you to the road where you turn left and at the end of the barn turn right through a stile and gate and walk along the path beside the wall on your right.

At the end of the second field the wooden stile is on your right. Cross the stream and ascend the field keeping the wall on your left. Over the brow go over a ladder stile and turn left and walk through a small farm on its left-hand side to the B6105 road. Turn right and left almost immediately afterwards over a stile and walk down the path beside the wall on your left to Swineshaw Reservoir. Bear right round the reservoir to its southern end and descend steps to a minor road. Turn right and walk past Keyford Cottage heading for Old Glossop, 1/2 mile away. Walk past the entrance to Shire Hill Hospital and down Bute Street. Turn left then right soon afterwards down a pedestrian lane—Dunne Lane. Turn right then left past the beautiful houses of Old Glossop to 'The Queens' where the walk began. Whilst I enjoy crossing moorland this particular walk past the reservoirs is a pleasant contrast to most walking in the Dark Peak.

Shorter walk—After walking up the fenced path to 'Open Country' and the site of a rifle range, keep straight ahead ascending the shoulder of the moorland on a distinct path. At the end of the second field the path keeps to the high ground with Shittern Clough on your left and Yellowslacks Brook on your right. Approximately 1/2 mile from the wall, on the edge of the clough (Yellowslacks), you reach a small stream and drainage channel. Here leave the path and by going on a compass bearing for Torside Castle you can cross this 3/4 mile section of moorland quite quickly. There are a few drainage channels at first but the surface is mostly cotton grass and bilberry. It is only when nearing Torside Castle that it becomes wet again. Keep to the left of the castle to gain the Pennine Way. Here you rejoin the main walk. Turn left and walk along the Pennine Way above Torside Clough.

START OF PATH AT OLD GLOSSOP FOR DOCTORS GATE.

THURLSTONE MOORS
- 10 miles

THURLSTONE MOORS
- 10 miles
- allow 4 hours.

  A616 near Flouch Inn—Far Swinden—A628—Soft-ley— Carlecotes—Townhead—Dunford Bridge—Windleden Lane—Gallows Moor—A628—Dog and Partridge Inn— Swinden Lane—A616.

O.S. 1:25,000 Outdoor Leisure Map—The Dark Peak.

Laybys on A616 road south of Flouch Inn. Grid Ref: SK202010.

ABOUT THE WALK - Flouch is the usual starting point for the Midhope Moors and the Derwent Valley. This walk goes in the opposite direction to explore moorland to the north of Flouch Inn. I had ear-marked this area for exploration and was rather surprised to find it so attractive and so peaceful. I saw only two hikers all day as I followed little used paths across the fields and moorland. I hope that you too enjoy this walk for a more pleasant one would be hard to find.

WALKING INSTRUCTIONS - From the car park turn right and walk down the side of the A616 road. At the first South Yorkshire bridlepath sign, turn right and follow a wide track. A 1/4 mile later the path—Cut Gate—turns left. Bear right here on a walled lane which you follow for the next 1/4 mile. The track goes through a gate before turning sharp right. Just beyond this turning leave the track and cross the field to a stile in front of the ruins of Far Swinden Farm. Keep to the right-hand side of the buildings to the track which you follow to the A628 road, 1/4 mile away. At the road turn right and moments later left and follow the signposted footpath to Hazlehead and Carlecotes. At first you walk down a walled lane but at its end you keep straight ahead on a path with the gritstone wall on your right. On nearing the railway line go through a gate and turn left and cross a bridge. Bear right on the other side down a sunken walled path to the infant river Don. Cross two footbridges and walk up the track to the left-hand side of Softley. The gentle rural scenery in this area is quite delightful.

At the road at Softley turn left and cross a bridge over a stream. Beyond go through a gate and diagonally cross the field following a faint footpath. It is well stiled and on nearing the left-hand side of the wood you walk along around it on a track to Carlecotes. At the road in the village turn left but before doing so it is worth turning right to see Carlecotes Hall and chapel. Follow the road 150 yards and turn left down the track for Eltock Farm—it is signposted - 'Public Footpath.' Descend the track for almost 1/4 mile an nearing a ruined farm the track turns sharp left. Here on your is the stone stile and path to Townhead. First you keep the wall on your left but after ascending a stile beside two trees you bear left to Townhead.

Gaining the road at Townhead turn left and descend to Dun Bridge, 1/2 mile away. There is no option but to road walk but it bring you interesting items—the Stanhope Arms Inn and entrance to the Woodhead tunnel. The tunnel was completed in 1845 and cost £200,000; it is 3 miles and 22 yds. long. Continue up the road passing a footpath on your right to Winscar Reservoir. Almost 1/2 mile later on Windleden Lane, turn left, as foot signposted, and follow the faint footpath around the right-hand of Upper Windleden Reservoir. Cross Board Clough and a ascending you reach a fence which should have a stile but hasn't! Stride over the fence and cross Woodland Clough via a stone bridge and follow the track on the left-hand side of the clough. The track reaches the A628 road on the right-hand side of South Nab, 1,511 ft.

Turn left at the road and walk along it past a layby car park to a footpath sign on your left. Leave the road here and follow a wide grass track which parallells the road through moorland. The views are extensive from here over the area you have walked through. After 1 1/2 miles you reach the A628 road opposite the Dog Partridge Inn. Turn left and 1/4 mile later turn right at the bridlepath sign, down a walled track. After another 1/4 mile the track t: sharp right down to a ford. Here as signposted you turn left at the walled Swinden Lane. For 1/2 mile the track is straight before bearing left. As you turn here you will recognise the ruined f you walked round at the beginning of the walk. You now re your starting out path which you follow back to the car park on A6 16 road . I will remember this walk for a long time—the peaceful countryside, the skylarks above, the call of the curlew, the star cry of the grouse and the views of villages and reservoirs. Yes, it is a walk that I enjoy very much.

FLOUCH INN.

UPPER WINDLEDEN RESERVOIR.

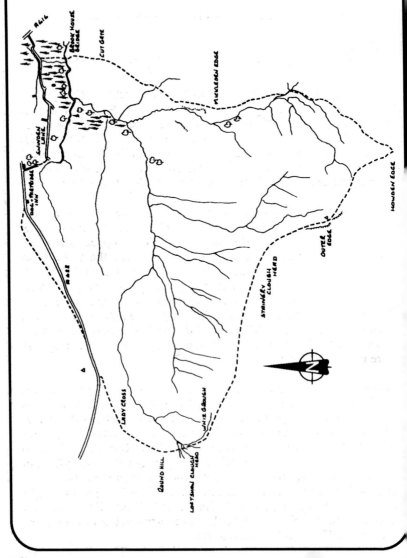

CUT GATE - 12 miles - allow 5 hours.

A616 nr. Flouch Inn—Brooke House Bridge—Cut Gate—Mickleden Edge—Howden Edge—Outer Edge—Stainery Clough Head—Whiz Grough—Loftshaw Clough Head— Round Hill—Lady Cross—A628—Dog and Partridge Inn —Swinden Lane—A616.

O.S. 1:25,000 Outdoor Leisure Map—The Dark Peak.

Layby on A616 near Flouch Inn. Grid Ref SK202010.

ABOUT THE WALK - At first the walk follows a wide distinct path— Cut Gate—to ascend to 1,700 ft. at Howden Edge. Here we leave the recognised path and maintain height contouring round the moorland above the Infant Derwent river. For our return we descend to the line of an old route and weave our way back to the Flouch area. A compass will be needed to cross the moors from whose summits you have extensive views over Bleaklow and the Derwent valley.

WALKING INSTRUCTIONS - From the layby turn right and walk down the side of the A616 road, towards Langsett. After 150 yards you reach the South Yorkshire bridlepath sign, on your right. Turn right here and walk along a wide track through the trees. After scarcely 1/4 mile you reach the footpath sign for 'Derwent'. Turn left here and continue along the hillside as you begin following Cut Gate. This is a former Packhorse route which linked Penistone with the Derwent valley. It is a good path all the way as you gradually ascend, walking along the top of Mickleden Edge and on across moorland to the summit of Howden Edge, north of Margery Hill. The view from here is a just reward.

Leave the main route and turn right, keeping to high ground, and head for the triangulation pillar on Outer Edge, a mile away. It is rugged walking across the heather and bilberry clad moorland. But as you walk along the grouse take to the air, a skylark sings above or a mountain hare bolts away from you. From Outer Edge keep to high ground as you curve round the peat groughs of Stainery Clough Head and on past Hoar Rock and another Howden Edge. Some 1/4 mile later, just past the delightfully named Whiz Grough, turn right across Loftshaw Clough Head to the summit of Round Hill. Here you descend to another old trade route—a saltway—at Lady Cross. Turn right and follow this to the A628 road.

Turn right and walk along the road passing a small car park on your left beneath South Nab. Some 200 yards later turn left and leave the road and follow the signposted bridlepath. The wide moorland track keeps away from the road and provides views across to Winscar Reservoir and Dunford. About 1l/2 miles along the track you reach the A628 road again opposite the Dog and Partridge Inn. Turn left and walk along the road for 1/4 mile, turning right at the bridlepath sign on the edge of a small wood. You follow a wide track and after barely 1/4 mile, as bridlepath signposted, turn left and walk along the walled 'Swinden Lane.' After 1/2 mile the track bears left which you follow as signposted. A 1/4 mile later you meet your starting out path on your right. Here you keep straight ahead retracing your steps back to the A616 road.

❋❋❋❋❋❋❋

UPPER DERWENT.

LADY CROSS.

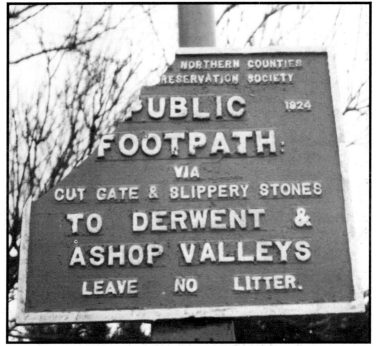

NORTHERN COUNTIES
PRESERVATION SOCIETY

PUBLIC 1924
FOOTPATH
VIA
CUT GATE & SLIPPERY STONES
TO DERWENT &
ASHOP VALLEYS
LEAVE NO LITTER.

CUT GATE PATH SIGN, NR. FLOUCH INN.

HOWDEN MOOR - 10 miles

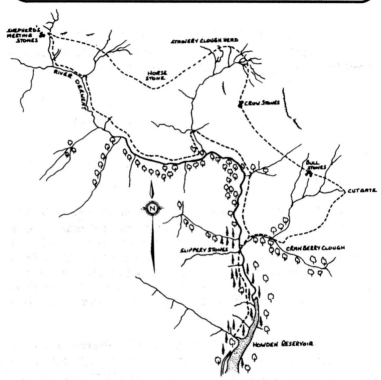

PACKHORSE BRIDGE AT SLIPPERY STONES.

HOWDEN MOOR - 10 miles - allow 4 1/2 hours.

 Howden Reservoir—Slippery Stones—Cranberry Clough —Cut Gate—Bull Stones—Crow Stones—Stainery Clough Head—Horse Stone—Shepherd's Meeting Stones —River Derwent—Slippery Stones—Howden Reservoir.

 O.S. 1:25,000 Outdoor Leisure Map—The Dark Peak.

End of road near northern end of Howden Reservoir. Grid Ref: SK168939.

ABOUT THE WALK - A short but deceptively tough walk. The hardest part is the first half as you walk across Howden Moors, maintaining high ground and passing several clusters of stones. The return walk is down beside the infant river Dove for 4 1/2 miles. I have done this walk in every season, even in winter. The walking then is harder with snow on the ground, I have also crossed the moorland section on skis and if there is sufficient snow on the ground this is by far the quickest and safest way !

WALKING INSTRUCTIONS - From the end of the road follow the wide footpath through the trees to Slippery Stones, 1/2 mile away. The packhorse bridge here across the infant river Derwent came from Derwent village which now lies flooded under Ladybower Reservoir. Across the bridge turn left and shortly afterwards right and begin ascending Cranberry Clough. The path is well defined. Cross the mouth of Bull Clough before ascending steeply for a short distance before the path eases off as you climb high above Bull Clough. Continue ahead for another 1/2 mile to the top of Cut Gate. Margery Hill and stones are on your right. Here you leave the path and begin contouring round the high ground. In bad weather you will have to take compass bearings. You can head for higher ground by aiming for the trig point on Outer Edge, but personally I prefer to aim first for Bull Stones.

You are now on moorland with deep groughs or drainage channels, so watch where you put your feet. Grouse wait until the last second and then take to the air with a startled cry. From Bull Stones aim for the wind carved Crow Stones, a little over 1/2 mile away. Across the valley from here can be seen the Horse Stone. It is almost a mile's

29

walking to the stone as you walk round Stainery Clough Head. From the Horse Stone maintain your high ground and head for the Shepherd's Meeting Stones a mile away. Once there you are close to the source of the Derwent. Across the valley is Barrow Stones, 1,920 ft.

From the Shepherd's Meeting Stones you can continue along a bit further to Swains Head, but I simply descend to the river Derwent and walk on its left-hand side. Now the hard part is over. At first there is only a faint path but the further down the river the wider it becomes. Eventually it becomes a wide track as you curve round Stainery Clough. A mile later you pass the path you walked up earlier to Cut Gate. Back at the bridge at Slippery Stones, cross over and retrace your steps to the road at Howden Reservoir. This walk serves as a good introduction to moorland walking and if the weather does deteriorate you know you only have to descend and return via the Derwent.

DESCENDING TO SLIPPERY STONES.

VIEW FROM ABBEY BANK TO DERWENT AND HOWDEN RESERVOIRS.

LADYBOWER INN SIGN.

ALPORT CASTLES - 9 miles

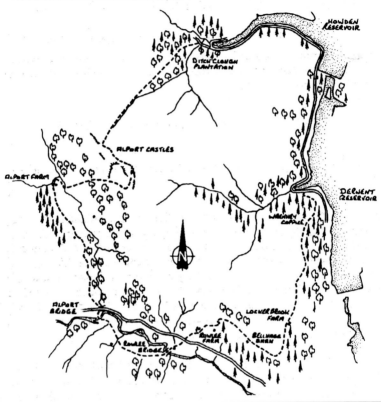

ALPORT CASTLES FARM.

ALPORT CASTLES - 9 miles - allow 3 1/2 hours.

  Alport Bridge—Alport Farm—Alport Castles—Ditch Clough Plantation—Howden Reservoir—Derwent Reservoir—Wrenhey Coppice—Lockerbrook Farm—Bellhagg Barn—Rowlee Farm—Rowlee Bridge—Alport Bridge.

O. S. 1:25, 000 Outdoor Leisure Map—The Dark Peak.

Car park: No official car park but parking room. Grid Ref: SK142896.

ABOUT THE WALK - Starting from the Snake road (A57) the walk takes you up Alport Dale before ascending to the summit of Alport Castles, a huge landslip. You cross open moorland and descend to one of the arms of Howden Reservoir which you walk beside together with part of Derwent Reservoir. For your return you ascend a rough track on the edge of woodland and gradually drop down to the river Ashop. It is a walk that combines all the scenic aspects of Peak District moorland walking—moors, reservoirs, cloughs, brooks, gritstone outcrops and deep valleys.

WALKING INSTRUCTIONS - On the left-hand side of Alport Bridge is the stile and signed footpath to Alport Dale. Ascend the path through the trees to the farm track. Here turn right and follow the track for a little over a mile to Alport Farm. On the first Sunday in July a Methodist 'Love Feast' is held here—a custom that dates back to the 17th century. Go through the farm and turn right along the track to the footbridge over the Alport river. Ahead you can see Alport Castles and the path that you now follow ascends to its right-hand side. It is steep climbing in places and on gaining the summit you turn left and walk along its top. As you do so you admire the view up the dale and down on to the landslip—one of the largest in Europe.

A 1/3 mile along the top you come to a stone wall; here you turn sharp right and walk along the path with the wall on your left-hand side. You soon begin to descend and after a mile enter Ditch Clough Plantation. A further 1/2 mile brings you to the road at the end of the western arm of Howden Reservoir. Turn right and walk along this road for the next two miles. It is delightful walking with the views across the water to moorland and in June the rhododendrons are at their best. Howden Reservoir was the first to be built in the valley and was completed in 1912. After walking past its dam wall you walk close to Derwent Reservoir, completed in 1916.

One mile from Howden dam wall the road curves round Ouzelden Brook. On the other side of the loop is the rough track and path sign, through Wrenhey Coppice to Lockerbrook Farm 11/2 miles away. It is a steady ascent at first before levelling off as you walk beside the plantation on your left. The views from the track do on to Derwent and Howden Reservoirs are exceptional. Continue past Lockerbrook Farm and a l/l mile later you reach a crossroads of paths. Turn right along your track as you walk past a wood on your left and past the solitary Bellhagg Barn. After the barn the track descends and switchbacks its way to Rowlee Farm. At the farm you are on a tarmac surface as you continue descending to the A57 road.

Cross the road and keep descending down a tarmac lane to Rowlee Bridge over the Ashop river. Ascend the track to your right as it curves round heading westwards before bearing right again an descending, to a ford and footbridge over the river. Ahead you can see Alport Bridge and the start of the walk. Alas. here the walk ends.

LADYBOWER RESERVOIR.

DERWENT RESERVOIR DAM WALL

J.J.CREBER

LOSE HILL - 8 miles

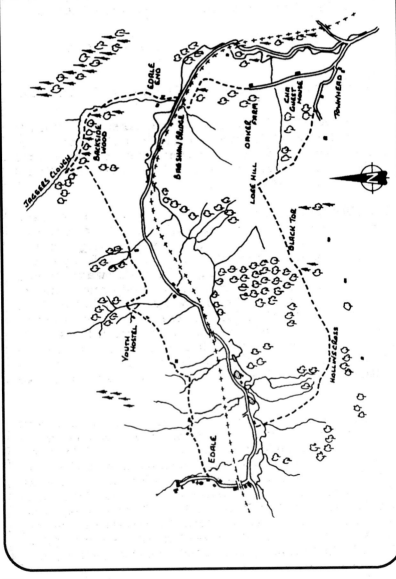

LOSE HILL - 8 miles - allow 3 1/2 hours.

 Edale—Hollins Cross—Back Tor—Lose Hill—Town-head—C.H.A. Guest House—Oaker Farm—Bagshawe Bridge—Edale End—Backside Wood—Jaggers Clough—Edale Youth Hostel—Edale.

O.S. 1:25,000 Outdoor Leisure Map—The Dark Peak.

At the road junction to Edale village. Grid Ref: SK124854.

ABOUT THE WALK - From Edale the route takes you immediately on to the 'Peakland Ridge' to the summit of Lose Hill. The views are extensive from here down on to the Hope Valley and across to the Kinder massif. For your return back to Edale you cross the Vale of Edale and contour round the vale.

WALKING INSTRUCTIONS - From the entrance of the car park, turn left and walk along the Hope road for about 1/4 mile. Upon nearing the first house on your right, turn right as signposted for Hollins Cross, and go through the stile. At first you walk along a farm track but after passing the farm on your left you follow a well trodden path up the valley side to Hollins Cross. On the ridge here is a circular cairn with reference map, in memory of Tom Hyett, of the Long Eaton Rambling Club. The views from here, especially down on to Castleton and to Mam Tor and its earthwork, are particularly rewarding. Turn left and keep to the wide path as it follows the ridge, firstly to Back Tor. Just where you begin the short steep ascent to the summit of Back Tor, you can take the horizontal path beneath to Tor and Lose Hill.

From the summit of Back Tor continue along the crest to the summit of Lose Hill. The hill across the valley is known as Win Hill and the two hills are reputed to have been named after a battle in the 7th century. The winners occupied Win Hill and the losers Lose Hill! Turn right from the summit and descend towards Townhead, a mile away. After 3/4 mile the path descends a rocky tree lined lane. Upon reaching the tarmac track to Townhead, turn left and then right soon afterwards to gain the lane to the C.H.A. Guest House. Turn left along the lane, passing the Guest House—Moor Gate— on your right in 1/4 mile. Continue along the lane and in another 1/4 mile you

37

you approach Oaker Farm. Instead of walking up to the farm go through the wooden stile on your left and follow the path beside the field boundary, keeping the farm on your right. The path is well stiled and after a further 1/4 mile swings to your left. At the end of this large field you reach a white painted ladder stile in Fiddle Clough.

Ascend the stile and turn right and walk down a farm track passing underneath a railway bridge to reach the Edale/Hope road. Turn right and almost immediately left through a wooden gate and descend the path to Bagshawe Bridge over the river Noe. Cross the bridge and walk along the farm road to Edale End, owned by the National Trust. One room of the building has been converted to a self-explanatory Information Centre. At the end of the building turn right and left shortly afterwards, as signposted. On the other side of the next gate, instead of following the wide track/path towards Crook-stone Barn, turn left as signposted for Jaggers Clough, and walk along the footpath beside the brook. This particular path weaves its way through Backside Wood and crosses the brook via a footbridge part way through. In June the wood floor is carpeted in bluebells. About 3/4 mile from Edale End you come opposite the wide track on your right which descends from near Crookstone Barn. Here you continue ahead a short distance before turning left and ascending out of the clough. On gaining the high ground the path curves sharp right as you begin heading for Edale. Ahead the Vale of Edale and the 'Peakland Ridge' stand out clearly. About 1/2 mile later the path divides at a footpath sign. Take the right fork for Edale Y . H. A. and Edale . The path hugs the valley side as it contours round small cloughs. At Lady Booth Brook the path curves to the hostel. On gaining the grounds turn left as footpath signposted, and walk in front of the buildings to the stile beyond.

The path continues to contour round the valley side for the next 1/2 mile. Then it turns sharp left and you descend two fields to the gate and track on your right. Walk along the track to the buildings at Ollerbrook Booth. At the western end of the buildings the path divides. Take the left fork to reach Edale on the right of Fieldhead, the National Park Information Centre and campsite. Turn left at the road and 1/4 mile later reach the car park on your left. As you walk along you pass the aptly named Rambler Inn on your right.

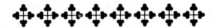

BACK TOR IN WINTER.

ROWLAND COTE - EDALE YOUTH HOSTEL.

CHINLEY CHURN - 8 miles

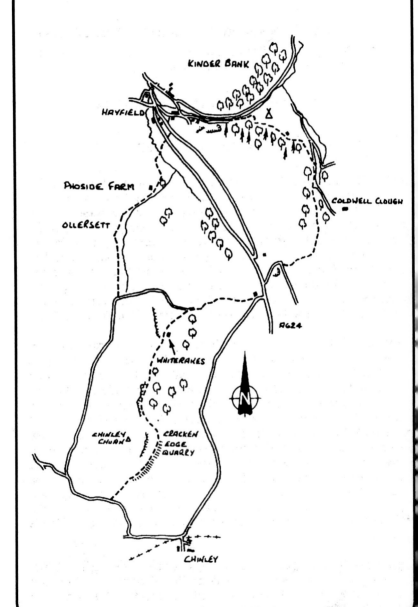

KINDER BANK

HAYFIELD

PHOSIDE FARM

OLLERSETT

COLDWELL CLOUGH

A624

WHITERAKES

N

CHINLEY CHURN

CRACKEN EDGE QUARRY

CHINLEY

CHINLEY CHURN - 8 miles - allow 3 1/2 hours.

    Hayfield (Kinder Bank) A624—Phoside Farm—Ollersett—Chinley Churn—Cracken Edge Quarry—Whiterakes—A624—Coldwell Clough—Kinder Bank (Hayfield).

O.S. 1:25,000 Outdoor Leisure Map—The Dark Peak.

Hayfield (Kinder Bank). Grid Ref: SK048869.

ABOUT THE WALK - Hayfield is the usual starting point for walking on to Kinder— to the Downfall or Edale Cross. However, to the south of Hayfield is a fascinating area of moorland around Chinley Churn. I first went walking here in the early 1960's and had the area to myself. Twenty years later, while checking this walk out, I again saw no one, despite it being a summer's day and a Sunday. Although a short walk there is a bit of climbing involved and the moorland should not be hurried for it provides an exceptional vantage point over to Kinder and Cheshire. Select a clear day and embark upon the walk on the western fringe of the National Park.

WALKING INSTRUCTIONS - From the car park cross the road and bridge over the river and turn right and walk down the road into the Hayfield Camping Club site. At the office and shop keep straight ahead along a footpath with the river on your immediate right. The path becomes a track then road and after 1/2 mile from the campsite you reach two rows of houses on your right. Here turn left and ascend the walled footpath on the left-hand side of a modern bungalow named 'Laneside'. At the top of the brief climb you come to a minor road opposite a house known as 'Langdale'. Turn left along the road and after 100 yards turn right down a walled lane beside a house named 'Moor Green'. Some 250 yards later you reach the A624 road. Go directly across the road, and as signposted for 'Phoside Public Bridleway', continue along a track to Phoside Farm scarcely 1/2 mile away.

Upon reaching the barn of Phoside Farm which was built in 1784, turn right through the wooden stile on the left of the gate. Turn left immediately afterwards, as signposted, 'Bridlepath—Ollersett'. Turn right almost immediately, again as signposted, and begin ascending the silver birch trees on a distinct footpath, keeping a small stream and mill pond on your left. At the end of the trees you reach a gate and open moorland. Continue climbing on a faint path to the line of a track. Here turn left still keeping the stream on your left-hand side. Some 300 yards later you meet another track coming in from your right. Again bear left heading due south across Ollersett moor. The track is well defined and you soon walk beside a gritstone wall on your right.

A 1/3 mile later, at the summit of the moorland, you reach a T junction of bridlepaths with a metal signpost. Here you turn right and walk along a walled track which soon swings left as you head once more southwards. For the next 3/4 mile you walk along this track as you begin descending to a minor road. As you lose height, Chinley Churn, 1,480 ft. high, with trig point, is 1/2 mile away on your left. In front of you and to your right are views over Cheshire. At the road turn left and walk past the entrance to Throstle Bank Farm. A 1/3 mile later after descending a short distance you reach a wooden stile on your left well before Dryclough Farm which you can see. The stile and path are not signed but it is readily noticeable. Over the stile you begin climbing on a distinct path as it weaves its way along the bottom and top of an earth bank. Soon you come to the abandoned remains of Cracken Edge Quarry. A little over 1/2 mile from the road you ascend steeply to your left up a diagonal path to the top of the main quarry slopes. The path is well defined and after the top of the incline it runs through shallow quarries on your left.

The views from here are rewarding, especially to Kinder. Approximately a mile from the road you begin descending a track running past Whiterakes on your right. The track curves round to your right to the farm track to Hills Farm. Turn right and follow the track, now heading due east to the A624 road, 1/2 mile away. At a metal gate you reach a tarmac road and the A624 road is a few yards away. The house on your left was built in 1841 by James and Mary Goddard, whose plaque can be seen on the front of the building. The house is often referred to as 'Peep o' day'. The front faces east and the first rays of the day hit the front and pass through a small glass window, 'the eye', above the doorway.

At the A624 road turn left and 100 yards later turn right on to a rough track on the right of Chinley Moor House. Just past a small quarry on your right you gain another walled track. Here turn right and left almost immediately and follow the public footpath signpost to 'Edale via Kinder Valley'. The path keeps a gritstone wall on your left. At a wooden gate you bear left and begin descending due north towards Coldwell Clough. The pathline is well defined. Upon reaching a tarmac road 1/2 mile later, turn left and, just over the brow of the hill and opposite a large white painted vertical stone, again turn left and follow the signposted bridleway to Highgate. At the end of the field you reach a wood; bear right here along a walled track around the wood's perimeter. As you descend towards the left-hand side of Stones House you can see the campsite and car park, 1/2 mile away. Towards the left-hand side of the campsite turn right through a stile and descend a series of stone steps, crossing the campsite to a footbridge. Bear right once across and ascend to the road. Turn right and the car park is a few yards away on your left.

"PEEP O' DAY" HOUSE.

KINDER DOWNFALL - 10 miles

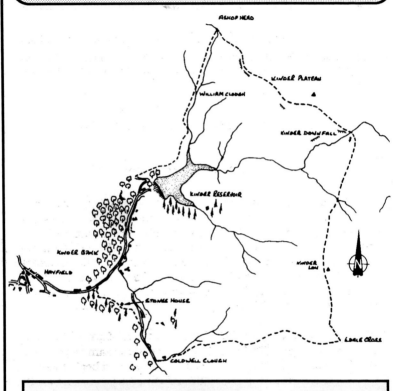

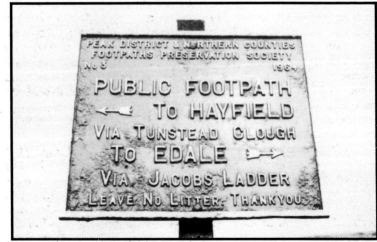

HAYFIELD - EDALE PATH SIGN.

KINDER DOWNFALL - 10 miles - allow 4 hours.

    Hayfield (Kinder Bank)—Kinder Reservoir—William Clough—Ashop Head—Kinder Plateau—Kinder Downfall—Kinder Low—Edale Cross—Coldwell Clough— Stones House—Kinder Bank (Hayfield).

O.S. 1:25,000 Outdoor Leisure Map—The Dark Peak.

Kinder Bank, Hayfield. Grid Ref: SK048869.

ABOUT THE WALK - A walk around the western edge of the Kinder plateau, providing one of the shortest routes to Kinder Downfall. However many times one visits the Downfall one is impressed by its setting. The deep sided clough with rocky ramparts and the trickle of water that floats down or is hurled back in windy conditions create a dramatic scene. Whatever the season the Downfall is spectacular. I always visit it in winter for then on an icy cold day it is at its best. Coated with ice and 120 feet high it is a glittering spectacle.

WALKING INSTRUCTIONS - From the car park turn left and walk northwards up the road. After 1/2 mile cross the stream on your right and follow a farm road. A 1/4 mile later turn left and begin following the path via Kinder Reservoir and William Clough to Ashop Head. The path zig-zags its way to 'Open Country' at Middle Moor. Here turn right and contour round the moorland side on a distinct path above the western side of Kinder Reservoir—Kinder Downfall can be seen directly ahead. Nearing the northern end of the reservoir you begin ascending steadily up William Clough—the hardest part of the walk. Some 1 1/4 miles later on the summit of Ashop Head, with Mill Hill summit 1,761 feet on your left, turn right and ascend the steep slope to the edge of the Kinder plateau. You are now on the Pennine Way.

The path is wide and well defined as you walk along the edge of the plateau towards Kinder Downfall, 1 1/2 miles away. In low cloud or mist this path should be treated with respect and you should always carry a compass. At the Downfall cross the small stream and keep to the edge of the peat moorland heading for Kinder Low, 2,077 ft., due north of here and about a mile away. A 1/2 mile due west of the Downfall and marked on the map is the Mermaid's Pool. It is said that to gain everlasting life you should sit beside the pool in the early hours of Easter Sunday morning. If you see the mermaid you will live for many years. Aaron Ashton from Hayfield came many times but never commented on whether he saw her or not. However, he died in 1835 aged 104!

Keep to the wide path heading north with good views to yo right down to Hayfield and Kinder Reservoir. The white triangu tion pillar on the 'summit' of Kinder Low is on your left. So afterWards bear right past the rocks of Swine's Back and descend the old medieval road from Hayfield to Edale Cross (G.R. SK077861). The cross was sometimes known as Champion Cross and is much older than the date on it— 1610. This refers to the tin it was restored. Here you turn sharp right and begin following this old packhorse route due west to Coldwell Clough, 1 1/2 miles away. The track is well used and walled.

Upon reaching the river Sett in Coldwell Clough turn right alo the metalled road and cross the river and ascend the other side. Upon reaching a tall white painted stone on your right opposite the second footpath sign on your left, turn left and cross the field to the edge of a small wood. Walk round the right-hand side of it along walled path as it descends and curves eastwards past Stones Hou on your right. A 1/4 mile from the house turn right and descend stel to cross Hayfield Camping Club site. Go through two gates ar cross a footbridge over the stream before turning right up to the road. A little way along here, on your left, is the car park.

THE MERMAID'S POOL.

CLIMBERS AT THE TOP OF KINDER DOWNFALL

KINDER DOWNFALL IN SUMMER

BARBER BOOTH
HORSESHOE - 10 miles

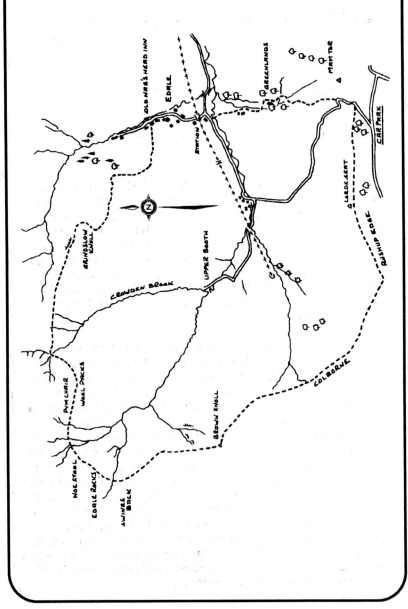

BARBER BOOTH HORSESHOE - 10 miles - allow 4 hours.

Rushup Edge—Colborne—Brown Knoll—Edale Head—Pym Chair—Wool Packs—Grindslow Knoll—Edale— Greenlands—Mam Nick—Rushup Edge.

O.S. 1:25,000 Outdoor Leisure Map—The Dark Peak.

At base of road to Mam Nick, beneath Rushup Edge. Grid Ref. SK124833.

ABOUT THE WALK - This route encircles the head of the Vale of Edale, keeping to the high ground above Barber Booth and Upper Booth and crossing a section of the Pennine Way alternative route above Jacob's Ladder. Having completed the high section the route crosses the valley floor via Edale and the renowned Old Nag's Head Inn. The final mile is the ascent of the valley side to the road immediately beneath Mam Tor. The walk, although short, is a good introduction to Kinder and moorland walking in the Peak District. If you set off along Rushup Edge by 10 a.m. you should reach the pubs in Edale by lunchtime!

WALKING INSTRUCTIONS - From the northern end of the car park ascend the steps and follow the path to the road to Mam Nick. Descend a short distance down the other side and turn left to follow the footpath along the crest of Rushup Edge. The edge is a magnificent viewpoint over the Kinder and Edale area. All the high ground encircling the valley is where you will be walking! The edge is also a popular take off point for hang gliders and as many as a dozen can be seen floating around on a Sunday. Keep to the wide path for about 3/4 mile to the first wooden stile on your right. Ascend this and begin making your way towards the triangulation pillar on Brown Knoll, 1,866 feet, about 11/2 miles away. In the past it was necessary to walk across this expanse of moorland by compass, but a path line can now be seen all the way. If the weather is bad or mist covered it is best to take a bearing to ensure a safe crossing. First you head almost due north over Colborne before heading north-west to Brown Knoll. From here you aim due north along a well defined path beside a wall to the bridleway from Upper Booth.

Cross the bridleway and ascend the slope above along a wide path to the gritstone wall beneath Swines Back. Turn right and keep on a well defined path as you now walk round the perimeter of Kinder Scout. After a short distance on your left are Edale Rocks and soon afterwards you reach the flat topped rock known as the Noe Stool. The top, gained by footholds, gives you a lofty perch from which to admire the surrounding area. Keep to the path as you swing due east around Edale Head to the rocks, Pym Chair. Ascend the rocks by their left-hand side and continue along the path through a large number of gritstone boulders known as Wool Packs. Beyond you descend gently to cross Crowden Brook passing Crowden Tower on your right. Now you are heading almost due east again as you aim for the prominent shape of Grindslow Knoll, 3/4 mile away. The actual path skirts around the knoll but a short ascent brings you to the summit cairn with views down on to Grindsbrook, Edale village and Mam Tor beyond. From Grindslow Knoll follow the wide path as it drops towards Edale. After half a mile you reach a gate with an unusual wooden ladder over it. Go over this, leaving the moorland behind you as you descend the fields, heading for the right-hand corner. Here you join the path into Edale beside a stream on the immediate left of Cooper's camp site. You reach Edale village opposite the Old Nag's Head Inn.

It is perhaps unfair but after that well-earned pint the final stage of the walk is uphill. However, from the Old Nag's Head you walk down through the village past the Information Centre on your left to the Hope road. Turn right and 50 yards later left along the farm road. Follow it for 1/2 mile as it winds its way to Greenlands. Leave the farm by its left-hand side following the sign—Mam Tor—and climb the wide track as it zig-zags its way to Mam Nick. Go up the road to rejoin your starting out path and descend to the car park.

EDALE CROSS - BEFORE WALL.

NAG'S HEAD INN, EDALE.

CROOK HILL - 12 miles

BLACK TOR

BRADFIELD GATE HEAD

DERWENT RESERVOIR

TIP'S TOMB

DERWENT DAM

LOCKERBROOK FARM

DERWENT EDGE

SALT CELLAR

WHITE TOR

OPEN HAGG

WHINSTONE LEE TOR

CROOKHILL FARM

ASHOPTON

A57

LADYBOWER RESERVOIR

CROOK HILL - 12 miles - allow 5 hours.

Ashopton—Crookhill Farm—Open Hagg—Lockerbrook Farm—Wrenhey Coppice—Derwent Dam—Shireowlers South Plantation—Green Sitches—Bradfield Gate Head— Cakes of Bread—Salt Cellar—White Tor—Wheel Stones —Whinstone Lee Tor—Ashopton.

O.S. 1.25,000 Outdoor Leisure Map—The Dark Peak.

Layby on A57 on the east side of Ashopton viaduct. Grid Ref: SK196864.

ABOUT THE WALK - Without fail, every New Year's Day in the 1970's I did a walk around Ladybower Reservoir and along Derwent Edge to let the New Year in. This walk is much longer and takes you along the other side of the valley over Crook Hill before crossing the valley to gain the Derwent Edge. I christened this route on New Year's Day, 1981, and although the weather was bad—gale force winds, driving snow and very cold— it was most enjoyable with a chicken leg, a hunk of Christmas cake and a bottle of whisky to enliven the proceedings!

WALKING INSTRUCTIONS - From the lay-by head westwards and cross Ashopton viaduct before turning right along the road up Derwent Dale. About 100 yards along here turn left through a small wooden gate and begin ascending diagonally to your right to Crookhill Farm. The path is not defined on the ground but after 400 yards you walk beside a wall on your right to the farm. Go through the gate between the buildings and through the farmyard to a farm track. Here turn left to a gate then right along a distinct grass track. Follow this gated track for the next half mile. As you walk along you have views down to Ladybower Reservoir and to Derwent Edge, your ultimate destination. Go over a wooden ladder stile and continue ascending to the summit of a rounded hill—the view back to Crook Hill is quite exceptional. The next mile is gentle descent to the footpath junction above Hagg Farm. For the final half mile you walk beside a large plantation on your right as you cross Open Hagg.

At the track and footpath junction turn right and follow the signposted path to Wrenhey Coppice, 1 1/2 miles. It is a track all the way and after 1/4 mile you pass Lockerbrook Farm on your right. Just beyond the farm you begin descending with further trees on your right. In the final stages you walk through a plantation (Wrenhey Coppice) and down a walled track to the road beside Derwent Reservoir. Turn right and walk down the road passing Gores Farm on your right. As you near Derwent Dam you pass Tip's Grave on your left. During the winter of 1953/54 Tip kept watch beside the body of her master who had died on Howden Moor. After fifteen weeks the body was found and Tip, although very weak, was nursed back to health. To commemorate this devotion this memorial was erected by public subscription.

Just beyond the dam wall turn left and descend along a footpath to a road bridge over the Derwent. Cross the bridge and follow the road for a short distance before turning left along another path which will bring you to the Water Board road beside the dam wall. Derwent Reservoir was completed in 1916 and was used in the making of the famous 'Dam Busters' film. Ascend a stile and walk along the track for half a mile, with the reservoir on your left. After half a mile a shallow valley on your right can be seen; here you turn right and walk through the trees of Shireowlers South Plantation to a wooden gate and 'Open Country'. The path line from here can be traced as you first climb due east before bearing left and ascending diagonally to the top of the high ground and a junction of footpaths. The footpath sign here indicates your route straight ahead to 'Bradfield Gate Head', 11/2 miles away. The path line is obvious and in 300 yards you ascend a wooden ladder stile and follow a grass track. You can see it ahead running beneath the high ground, across Green Sitches to Derwent Edge south of Back Tor.

On gaining Derwent Edge turn right and follow a wide and distinct footpath, as you gradually descend for the next three miles. As you go downhill you have further views of where you have walked— especially of Crook Hill. As you walk along you have a whole string of interesting rock shapes to see. In walking order they are the Cakes of Bread, Salt Cellar, White Tor and Wheel Stones. On reaching Whinstone Lee Tor at a junction of footpaths, two miles from Bradfield Gate Head, turn sharp right and go down to a stone wall. Here turn left and walk beside it along a grass track to a gate into a plantation. Use the gate on the left of the main gate and walk through the trees and descend to another gate. Here turn right and walk down the rough track past the houses on your left to the road (A57). The layby is opposite on your left. Regrettably another walk ends. The Ladybower Inn is just 1/2 mile up the A57 road towards Sheffield on your left-hand side.

WHEEL STONES.

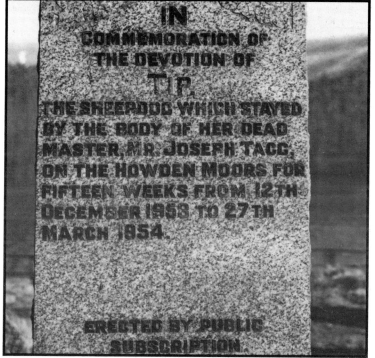

IN
COMMEMORATION OF
THE DEVOTION OF
TIP
THE SHEEPDOG WHICH STAYED
BY THE BODY OF HER DEAD
MASTER, MR. JOSEPH TAGG,
ON THE HOWDEN MOORS FOR
FIFTEEN WEEKS FROM 12TH
DECEMBER 1953 TO 27TH
MARCH 1954.

ERECTED BY PUBLIC
SUBSCRIPTION.

TIP'S GRAVE.

THE HOPE VALLEY - 7 miles

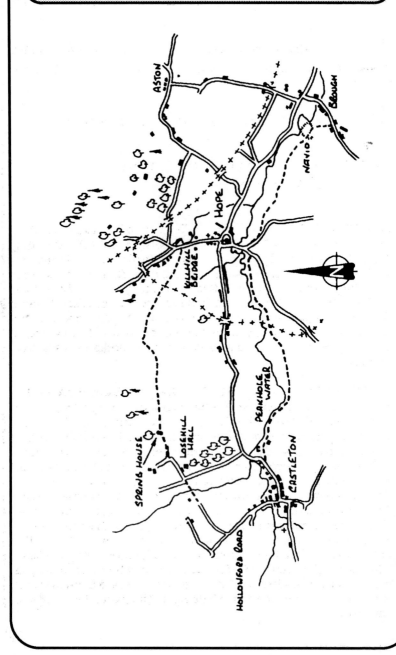

THE HOPE VALLEY - 7 miles - allow 2 1/2 hours.

 Castleton—Hollowford Road—Losehill Hall—Spring House—Killhill Bridge—Aston—Brough—Navio— Peakshole Water— Castleton.

 O.S. 1:25,000 Outdoor Leisure Map—The Dark Peak.

Western side of Castleton off A625 road.
Grid Ref: SK149830.

ABOUT THE WALK - The Hope Valley is one of the scenic wonders of Derbyshire and is flanked by high moorland and hills. Running along the valley is a small river, which at Castleton is a stream but within five miles becomes a wide flowing river. Rather than ascend on to the surrounding heights this walk takes you along both sides of the valley floor via two small hamlets and an important Roman fort—Navio. You also walk in both limestone and gritstone country and see from a distance contrasting works of man—the impressive Norman Peveril Castle and a modern cement works with massive chimney.

WALKING INSTRUCTIONS - From the car park leave by its northern end and walk beside a small stream, before bearing right between the houses to Hollowford Road. Turn left and 1/3 mile later turn right along the track in front of Hollowford Centre. At the end of the gravel track you reach a gate and cattle grid. Cross the grid and then turn right following a footpath across the fields to the road beside Losehill Hall, the National Park Study Centre, 1/4 mile away. The path is defined and well stiled. At the road continue ahead past Losehill Hall. Where the road turns left to Field's Farm keep straight ahead across three fields, keeping the field boundary on your immediate right, to Spring House. Bear right down the lane here for a few yards past the garden of a modern house before turning left and crossing the field, with its hedge on your immediate left. The path is well stiled as you cross eight fields. After two fields you cross the field boundary and keep the fences on your immediate right. The path later swings to your left.

At the end of eight fields you reach a prominent sign indicating the path to Lose Hill and Mam Tor to your left. Here you turn right and descend the fields to Killhill, on the northern side of the village of Hope, and the Edale Road. The path is well defined and at all footpath junctions you keep straight ahead. To cross the railway line from Hope cement works, you have stiles and a concrete footbridge. Seven fields from here turn left to the houses at Killhill.

Cross the Edale-Hope road and walk down a small lane and cross Killhill Bridge over the river Noe. Just past the house on your right, turn right along a lane following the signposted path—'Aston'. You walk underneath the main railway line from Sheffield to Manchester and reach the road to Aston village 1/2 mile later. Turn left and follow the delightful sunken road for 1/2 mile through this quiet unspoilt hamlet.

Turn right at the first road junction and descend to the floor of the Hope Valley and the A625 road. Overlooking the road junction is a particularly fine building which dates back to 1578. As you descend you have extensive views over the valley, to Castleton and Bradwell, and behind you is Win Hill. At the A625 road turn left and opposite the aptly named Traveller's Rest Inn, whose sign depicts a couple of resting hikers, turn right on to the B6049 road for Brough and Bradwell. Part of this road runs along the line of Batham Gate, a Roman road. In little over 1/2 mile, immediately after Burghwash Bridge, turn right and follow the signposted footpath—'Hope, I mile.' The path is clear and after ascending a wooden ladder stile you walk across the area of the Roman fort known as Navio.

The fort, originally built about 80 A.D., has been excavated several times this century. From excavations it would appear that there were three major building periods and that Navio became the control fort for the Peak District and was occupied well into the 4th century. It is a shame that on the surface little can be seen, apart from definite mounds outlining the basic shape. At the end of the fort area you cross a wooden footbridge. The path then curves its way high above the river and campsite to the road on the southern side of Hope. Turn right and descend the road to a road junction. Turn left and 100 yards later turn right and go through a stile . follow the distinct path near Peakshole Water to Castleton miles away. After 1/2 mile the path crosses the railway line from cement works on your left. In a further 1/2 mile you walk beside the stream before leaving it to reach Castleton on its eastern side. Turn left and follow the A625 road into the centre of Castleton. The park is a little further on your right.

HOPE/NAVIO/CASTLETON PATH SIGN.

PATH TO NAVIO AT BROUGH - WIN HILL IN DISTANCE.

59

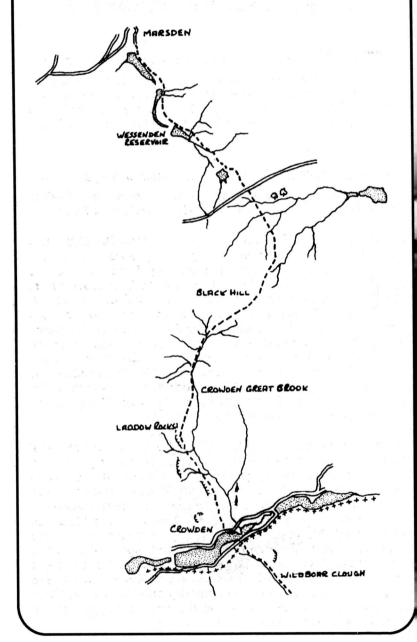

MARSDEN TO EDALE
- 25 miles
- allow 6 to 12 hours.

Marsden—Wessenden Reservoir—Wessenden Head— Pennine Way—Black Hill—Crowden Great Brook— Laddow Rocks—Crowden—Wildboar Clough—Bleaklow Head—Devil's Dike—Snake Road (A57)—Featherbed Top—Ashop Clough shooting cabin (ruins)—The Edge— Kinder Scout—Grinds Brook—Edale.

O.S. 1:50,000 series No. 110—Sheffield to Huddersfield—covers the whole walk. O. S. 1:25,000 series Outdoor Leisure Map—The Dark Peak—covers the section from Wessenden Head Moor to Edale.

ABOUT THE WALK - Known as the 'classic' walk of the High Peak, this famous bogtrot was first completed by Ross Evans. Cecil Dawson, a Manchester cotton merchant, popularised the route. It has always been a challenge walk demanding the highest standards. Fred Heardman, in the early 1920s, did the first double walk but it wasn't until 1953 that the double was completed in under thirteen hours. Since then times have been consistently broken. In December 1980 Rob Pearson successfully crossed from Marsden to Edale in an amazing 2 hrs. 39 mins. Harry Buckley would appear to have walked it more often than anyone for in September 1953 he completed his 116th solo crossing! An annual marathon known as 'Tanky's Trog' is held organised by Sheffield climber and shop owner, Tanky Stokes. In 1980 there were a record 142 starters.

Whilst the route does have this challenge side I mention it all out of interest, for the walk across this moorland mass is very hard and dangerous. Given good conditions and good weather it can be completed comfortably in between six and twelve hours. However, as so often happens on these moors, the conditions can be atrocious both weatherwise and underfoot. It is then extremely hard and it is best to leave the moor and descend to the valley. For your own safety you must be properly clad and experienced with map and compass. Whilst the route does follow part of the well trodden Pennine Way it takes more direct lines on to the moors in places. Here you will need to go on compass bearings. Select your day with care and even have a support party waiting for you at the road crossings, such as Crowden and Snake Road.

MARSDEN TO EDALE
- 25 miles - *SOUTHERN HALF*

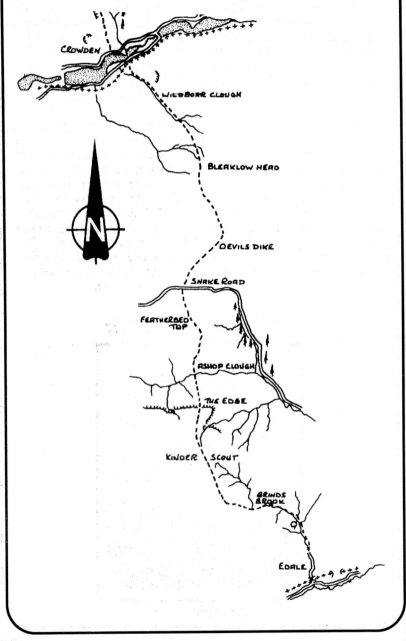

WALKING INSTRUCTIONS - From Marsden, near the Youth Hostel, you walk beside four reservoirs—Butterley, Blakeley, Wessenden and one near the road (A635) at Wessenden Head. For this section you have been following the alternative route of the Pennine Way. At the road you join the Pennine Way proper and follow it for the next seven miles to Crowden. Now you really enter the world of peat as you cross Black Hill, 1,908 ft., known for its quagmire. Heading almost due north from here you begin descending Crowden Great Brook and over Laddow Rocks to Crowden. From Crowden you leave the Pennine Way and make a more direct ascent to Bleaklow Head via Wildboar Clough. Bleaklow is the crux to the walk and in mist or low cloud it can be a hard route-finding problem.

At Bleaklow Head you rejoin the Pennine Way and follow it past Hern Clough and Devil's Dike to the Snake Road (A57). Here you leave the Pennine Way again and make a direct ascent on to Kinder towards the Fairbrook Naze side of The Edge. This is a cruel section and will really test your muscles as you cross Featherbed Top and descend Upper Gate Clough to the ruins of the shooting cabin in Ashop Clough. Now you ascend steeply up Black Ashop Moor to the Edge. Kinder is before you as you make your way across the peat trough plateau to the top of Grindsbrook. Although tired you now know you are on the final lap. A little over two miles descent of Grindsbrook brings you to Edale and the welcome sight of the Nag's Head Inn. There you can rest with pride after your tough walk.

❋ ❋ ❋ ❋ ❋ ❋ ❋ ❋

BOGTROTTING!

KINDER CIRCUIT - HIGH LEVEL ROUTE - 18 miles

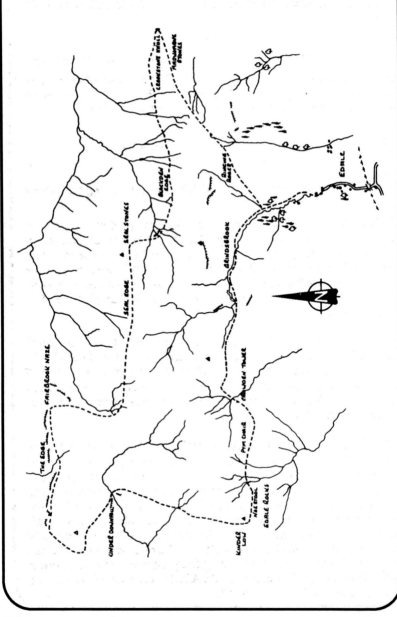

KINDER CIRCUIT - HIGH LEVEL ROUTE - 18 miles - allow 7 to 8 hours.

 Edale—Grindsbrook—Crowden Tower—Pym Chair Noe Stool—Edale Rocks—Kinder Low—Kinder Down—The Edge— Fairbrook Naze—Seal Edge—Seal Stones—Blackden Edge—Crookstone Knoll—Madwoman Stones—Ringing Roger—Edale.

 O.S. 1:25 000 Outdoor Leisure Map—The Dark Peak.

At the road junction to Edale village. Grid Ref: SK124854

ABOUT THE WALK - The Kinder plateau lying at a height of around 2,000 feet enables a magnificent circuit to be made around its perimeter. It is a gruelling walk and a good eight hours are needed. For me it is one of the most interesting walks on Kinder for you see in one fell swoop its differing features. At the end of the walk your muscles will be strained but you will be more than satisfied at completing it.

I try and do the circuit clockwise, for anti-clockwise is the 'Devil' Way'. It does mean that you are at your furthest point while still fresh. Another of the advantages of the walk is that once you are over half way you can quickly retreat back to Grindsbrook if time or fitness become a problem. Whatever you do you can be assured of an exceptional walk on Kinder.

WALKING INSTRUCTIONS - From Edale walk through the village and up the Pennine Way . it climbs up the right-hand side of Grindsbrook Clough. Climb to the top of Grindsbrook before bearing left and following the fool path across Edale Moor to Crowden Tower and on through the remarkably lifelike stones known as Wool Packs. The path crosses the top of Edale Head passing Noe Stool. Soon afterwards bear right past Edale Rocks to the trig point on Kinder Low (2,077 ft.). Just west of here you pick up the alternative route of the Pennine Way as you continue along the perimeter with views down onto Hayfield and Kinder Reservoir. A little over a mile from the trig point you reach Kinder Downfall.

Continue on the Pennine Way, cross the stream feeding the downfall and now head north-westerly. Where the Pennine Way leaves the perimeter you keep right, maintaining height as you head due east along the rocks on the top of The Edge. In under two mile you reach the summit of Fairbrook Naze with its views down onto Ashop Clough and across to the Snake Road. Turn sharp right and head southwards to cross the head of Fairbrook Clough. You now head east again as you walk along the top of Seal Edge, where several of the stones look like seals resting on rocks. At the trig point on Seal Stones, continue southwards again to go round the head of Blackden Brook.

Head eastwards once more as you walk along the narrow plateau past Blackden Edge and on to the trig point on Crookstone Knoll, your most eastern point. You now go westwards, almost retracing your steps, as you cross Madwoman's Stones and on to the trig point 1,937 feet 1/2 mile away. From here I begin my exit of the plateau by heading to the left, southwards, to Ringing Roger an the path down to Grindsbrook. Turn left in the bottom and Edale and the car park are not far away.

TOP OF GRINDSBROOK

KINDER'S THREE WISE MEN.

THE RAMBLER INN, EDALE.

KINDER CIRCUIT - LOW LEVEL ROUTE - 24 miles

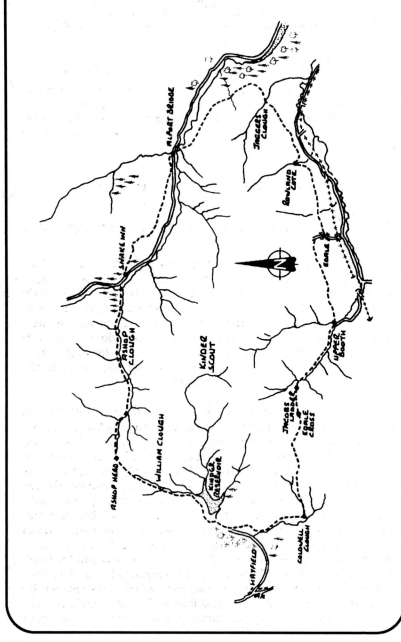

KINDER CIRCUIT - LOW LEVEL ROUTE - 24 miles - allow 10 hours.

  Edale—Ollerbrook Booth—Rowland Cote Youth Hostel —Jagger's Clough—Crookstone Barn—Blackley Clough —Alport Bridge—Hayridge Farm—Oyster Clough— Snake Inn—Ashop Clough— Ashop Head—William Clough—Kinder Reservoir—Kinder Bank (Hayfield)— Coldwell Clough—Edale Cross—Jacob's Ladder—Upper Booth—Edale.

O.S. 1:25,000 Outdoor Leisure Map—The Dark Peak.

At the road junction to Edale village. Grid Ref: SK124854.

ABOUT THE WALK - The most mountainous circuit in the Peak District! This really is a hard walk with more than 4,000 feet of climbing. En route you see the finest Dark Peak scenery and entirely encircle the Kinder plateau without actually walking upon it. You cross several roads which make easy 'retirement' points and also enable you to have a support party ready. I usually do the walk anti-clockwise for when you descend from Edale Cross into the Vale of Edale, you have earned that view. A look at the map indicates the route but the following are a few comments.

WALKING INSTRUCTIONS - From the car park walk up the Edale road and a little way past the entrance to Fieldhead, the National Park Information office, turn right and follow the path to Ollerbrook Booth. Head east from here and half a mile later bear left and follow the path to Edale Y.H.A. —- Rowland Cote. Walk in front of the hostel and around Lady Booth Brook and continue gently ascending before dropping to Jagger's Clough a mile away. Here you go up a wide path to a crossroads of footpaths well to the right of Crookstone Barn. Turn left following a bridlepath around Blackley Clough and down to the footbridge over Ashop river, near Alport Bridge. Cross the A57 at Alport Bridge and ascend the path on its left-hand side to the track to Alport Farm. Turn left and descend to Hayridge Farm. Here turn right and follow the line of a Roman road which rises around the southern side of Cowms Moor and falls to Oyster Clough. A steep ascent follows before dropping through trees to the A57 road north of the Snake Inn. Turn left down the road and leave it 1/4 mile later and follow the path up Ashop Clough. The Snake Inn is a little way down the road on your left.

The path up Ashop Clough keeps to the right-hand side of the valley. At the top of Ashop Head keep straight ahead and descend William Clough and walk round the northern side of Kinder Reservoir. All the time you have excellent views of Kinder and Downfall. At Farlands Booth follow the path via Hill House Farm to Coldwell Clough. Here you turn left and begin your final major ascent as you follow the old packhorse route to Edale Cross. A little beyond here towards Jacob's Ladder, you get the view down on to the Vale of Edale with Kinder on the left and Mam Tor and the Peakland ridge on your right.

Descend Jacob's Ladder and continue down the track to Upper Booth. Here turn left and follow the path across the fields to Edale 1 1/2 miles away. Turn right in the village and retrace your steps back to the car park. Sadly that ends the finest walk in the Peak District.

ASHOP CLOUGH PATH SIGN NR SHAKE PASS INN.

SNAKE PASS INN.

LOOKING UPTO FAIR BROOK NAZE.

71

THE DERWENT WATERSHED
WALK - 40 miles - *EAST HALF*

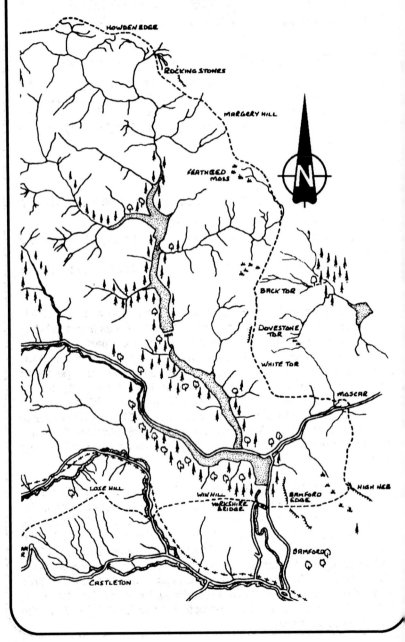

THE DERWENT WATERSHED WALK - 40 miles - allow 12 to 15 hours,

Yorkshire Bridge (Bamford)—Win Hill—Lose Hill— Mam Tor—Rushup Edge—Brown Knoll—Kinder Downfall—Mill Hill— Moss Castle—Snake Road—Bleaklow Stones—Swains Head— Howden Edge—Rocking Stones —Margery Hill—Featherbed Moss— Back Tor—Dovestone Tor—Moscar—High Neb—Bamford Edge—York- shire Bridge.

O.S. 1:25,000 Outdoor Leisure Map—The Dark Peak (covers all the route apart from Stanage Edge area).
- O.S. 1:25,000 Pathfinder Series Sheet No. SK28/38 details the Stanage area.
O.S. l:50,000 series No. 110—Sheffield and Huddersfield (covers whole route).

ABOUT THE WALK - The is the toughest walk in the Peak District. It is exhausting and requires determination. The crux is in the latter half as when you reach the Snake road the hardest part is to follow. Make sure you are fit, fully conversant with a compass and that someone knows when and where you are going and are expected to return. The walk was first completed in 1918 by a party led by Eustace Thomas- they took 11 hours 39 minutes. This was a very good time and one should allow between 12 and 15 hours to complete it. The route is best tackled between May and September. The first time I did the route was one early October day and I completed the walk in 12 hours.

WALKING INSTRUCTIONS - Start at Yorkshire Bridge in Bamford, situated on the minor road from Bamford to Thornhill. Where the road crosses the bridge before turning sharp left towards Thornhill, turn right up the track a short distance to the path for Win Hill on your left. The path is well defined but steep and the summit of Win Hill is rocky and reminiscent of North Wales. Descend towards Thornhill Brink before going down sharply towards Fullwood Stile Farm. Continue down to the main road from Hope to Edale, following this for 200 yards towards Hope before branching right along the road to Losehill Farm.

THE DERWENT WATERSHED WALK - 40 miles - *WEST HALF*

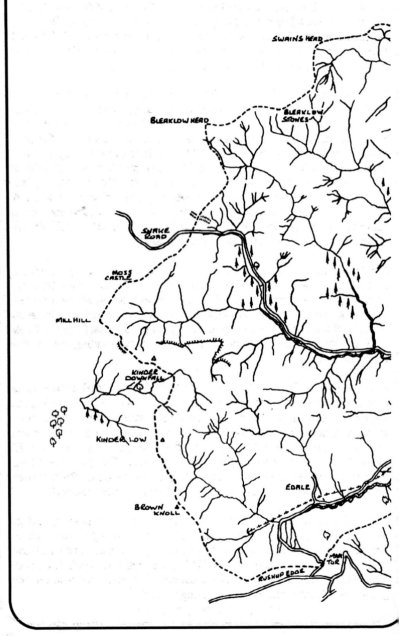

Near the farm turn right up a grassy track towards the summit of Lose Hill. On the summit is a cairn with a metal top which names and indicates various places and peaks in the neighbourhood. You will come to know most of them as the day proceeds. The ridge walk to Mam Tor is easy and pleasant, both Back Tor and Hollins Cross being passed. At Mam Tor descend sharply to the minor road to Edale, crossing the road and climbing Rushup Edge. After two miles turn right at a signpost towards Barber Booth, and after a short distance turn left or take a compass bearing for Brown Knoll. The bog-trot which will stay with you much of the way starts here.

From Brown Knoll descend slightly towards Edale Cross. Keep to the high ground and edge of the plateau, passing Kinder Low on your right-hand side. There is a well-marked footpath beside the Kinder Downfall and this is a good stopping point. Continue round the plateau along a clear path towards Mill Hill, descending steeply to the Snake path before the ascent of Mill Hill begins. Turn sharp right at Mill Hill towards Moss Castle and the Snake road; it is at its highest point (1,680 ft.) here. Several wooden poles spaced at regular intervals are a guide along this faint path, some of them being marked 'H 90'. The Snake road and the half-way point is reached; this is also a good rendezvous for a support party.

For the next 15 miles you will cross a huge, serrated plateau on compass bearings. Bleaklow is an appropriate name for this expanse. From the Snake road lies an easy walk to Devil's Dike followed by a slow ascent to Bleaklow Head. Compass is needed for Bleaklow Hill, Bleaklow Stones, Swains Head, Featherbed Moss, Howden Edge and the Rocking Stones, when at last you are moving out of this horrible region.

More bogland is crossed towards Margery Hill and Featherbed Moss, a semi-circular route round Abbey Brook to Back Tor. The worst is over here. Continue along Derwent Edge, passing many rock outcrops with odd-shaped stones. Dovestone Tor and the 'Salt Cellar' are passed. Turn left near White Tor, a signpost indicates Moscar. It IS possible to continue along the edge past White Tor passing Wheel Stones on the left before curving sharp left to Moscar. Both routes converge before the main Sheffield-Glossop road is reached.

Cross the road and follow the well-worn path along Stanage Edge. When you reach the trig point on High Neb, turn right down one of the many paths to the road and trees at Dennis Knott. Turn right and walk down the road past Bamford Edge to the A6013 road. The Yorkshire Bridge Inn is on your right! Descend the road to your left to the Yorkshire Bridge where the walk began at dawn

SALT CELLAR - DERWENT EDGE.

BACK TOR SUMMIT.

PEAK DISTRICT & NORTHERN COUNTIES
FOOTPATHS PRESERVATION SOCIETY

NO. 86   1935.

**PUBLIC
FOOTPATH**

VIA DERWENT EDGE
⬅ TO DERWENT

PLEASE KEEP TO THE PATH AND
LEAVE   NO   LITTER

BEYOND THE COTTAGE THE
PATH BEARS LEFT BEFORE
RUNNEL IS REACHED

DERWENT RESERVOIR

NATURAL HISTORY NOTES

The moorland areas of Kinder and Bleaklow are fascinating places and have several special features. The following are some of them.

 FLORA:

Peat: Kinder and Bleaklow provide ideal locations for peat to form; the fact that they are waterlogged means that bacterial activity cannot break down the dead plant remains. The peat began forming 7,500 years ago from sphagnum moss. When this plant dies the next growth appears on top forming the very thick surface we see today. The surface vegetation is mostly cotton grass, bilberry and cloudberry and is a result of man's influence by draining and burning the area. Burning has been carried out for many centuries and some charcoal found in the peat has been carbon dated to 1300 A.D. Sphagnum moss, because of its absorbent qualities, was used during World War I in hospitals as a surgical dressing. From pollen grains taken from the peat it has been possible to record chronologically the vegetational history of the area:

> **9,000 B.C.**—Only trees such as rowan, willow and juniper existed.
> **8,200 B.C.**—Warmer climate. Birch, juniper and pine growing.
> **7,600 B.C.**—Warmer with oak, elm and hazel trees growing.
> **5,600 B.C.**—Decline in tree pollen. The climate warmer and drier and peat growth stationary.
> **600 B.C.**—Climate like today's—cooler and wetter. Peat grew rapidly. Drainage channels began to form.

Cotton Grass: White hairy heads that wave in the breeze are seen in May and June. Common cotton grass has five or six heads at the top of each stem. Hair's Tail cotton grass has only one head.

Cloudberry: Usually grows above 2,000 ft. Has kidney-shaped leaves and the stems mainly spread underground. The flowers appear in midsummer and both male and female plants have their own flower. The fruit is edible and like a yellow raspberry.

Bilberry: Sometimes known as whortleberry. The shrub grows to about two feet tall and has green bell-shaped leaves. The round blue-

-black berries appear in July.

Juniper: Can be seen growing in several areas. Instead of being upright the branches spread along the ground. The actual trunk can be quite thick.

 # BIRDS:

Red Grouse: Native and unique to Britain. Grows to about 15 inches and has a red/brown body with dark wings and tail. Lives largely on ling heather. The nest is usually a scrape in the ground lined with heather or grass. The female lays between four and nine eggs in April or May. The eggs are white with dark blotches.

Curlew: Often seen and heard on the moors during the summer. It is at twenty-two inches our largest wader and has a long curving beak. Nests on the moor and lines its nest with grass or heather. Usually four eggs are laid, brown with dark blotches.

Ring Ouzel: Visitor to Britain during the summer months and about the same size as a thrush. Black in colour with a white 'bib' on the breast. They can often be seen singing from a rock. Their diet is both animal and vegetable food.

MOUNTAIN HARE: Often known as blue hares as their fur has a bluish appearance in spring and autumn. Although often seen during the summer months, they come into their own in winter and are easily recognised. Their coats turn white and only their ear tips remain black. They are very conspicuous in winter for there are very few days when snow is actually lying on the moors.

SUGGESTED FURTHER READING

High Peak by Eric Byne and Geoffrey Sutton. Secker & Warburg,

Dark Peak Wrecks by Ron Collier and Ron Wilkinson. Barnsley Chronicle, 1979. (Two volumes).

High Ground Wrecks by David J. Smith. Midland Counties Publications, 1989.

Freedom to Roam by Howard Hill. Moorland Publishing Ltd., 1980.

Rock Climbing Guides to Kinder, Bleaklow, Laddow, Chew and Saddleworth Moors.

☆☆☆☆☆★☆

DESCENDING TO DERWENT RESERVOIR.

REMEMBER AND OBSERVE THE COUNTRY CODE

 Enjoy the countryside and respect its life and work.

 Guard against all risk of fire.

 Fasten all gates.

 Keep your dogs under close control.

 Keep to public paths across farmland.

 Use gates and stiles to cross fences, hedges and walls.

  Leave livestock, crops and machinery alone.

 Take your litter home - pack it in; pack it out.

 Help to keep all water clean.

Protect wildlife, plants and trees.

STOP *Take special care on country roads.*

81

THE HIKER'S CODE

- 🌼 *Hike only along marked routes - do not leave the trail.*

- 🌼 *Use stiles to climb fences; close gates.*

- 🌼 *Camp only in designated campsites.*

- 🌼 *Carry a light-weight stove.*

- 🌼 *Leave the trail cleaner than you found it.*

- 🌼 *Leave flowers and plants for others to enjoy.*

- 🌼 *Keep dogs on a leash.*

- 🌼 *Protect and do not disturb wildlife.*

- 🌼 *Use the trail at your own risk.*

- 🌼 *Leave only your thanks and footprints - take nothing but photographs.*

A FEW NOTES ON WALKING IN THE HIGH COUNTRY

Walking should be a pleasurable experience and all the walks in this book are geared to ensure maximum enjoyment. They are circular, through diverse scenery and have much of interest to see on the way. To get even better enjoyment the following are a few guidelines.

Blisters: Always ensure that your boots are comfortable and broken in. Your socks should be close fitting and have no kinks in them. Blisters happen without warning and are a 'fact of life'. If you get one, cover the area well with moleskin or second skin and ensure that your boots are laced reasonably tight. Don't prick them as this can cause infection or for the skin to rub off which is even more harmful.

Walking clothing: Wear a shirt, pullover and windjacket as a basic rule with either corduroy trousers or walking breeches. Do not wear jeans as these can be a death trap if conditions worsen. In winter a duvet or a thinsulate jacket will keep you warm in the coldest weather. Gloves and hat are also a must. In the summer a pair of shorts is quite adequate.

Emergency: Carry a whistle and torch and know the International Distress Signal of six blasts in a minute with a minute silence between. The reply is three blasts in a minute with a minute silence between. If you have to alert the police give them full details and a grid reference of where the injured person is. It is also useful to carry a bar of Kendal mint cake or some chocolate.

Walking speed: There is no need to rush when walking, a pleasant steady pace is all that is required. As a basic rule an average person will walk 2 1/2 to 3 miles in one hour or ascend 2,000 feet in one hour. When climbing uphill adopt a slow, steady pace and keep it up. Descending you can relax and quicken your pace.

EQUIPMENT NOTES

- Some personal thoughts

BOOTS - *preferably with a full leather upper, of medium weight, with a vibram sole. I always add a foam cushioned insole to help cushion the base of my feet.*

SOCKS - *I generally wear two thick pairs as this helps minimise blisters. The inner pair are of loop stitch variety and approximately 80% wool. The outer are a thick rib pair of approximately 80% wool.*

WATERPROOFS - *for general walking I wear a T shirt or cotton shirt with a cotton wind jacket on top. You generate heat as you walk and I prefer to layer my clothes to avoid getting too hot. Depending on the season will dictate how many layers you wear. In soft rain I just use my wind jacket for I know it quickly dries out. In heavy or consistant rain I slip on a neoprene lined gagoule, and although hot and clammy it does keep me reasonably dry. Only in extreme conditions will I don overtrousers, much preferring to get wet and feel comfortable. I never wear gaiters!*

FOOD - *as I walk I carry bars of chocolate, for they provide instant energy and are light to carry. In winter a flask of hot coffee is welcome. I never carry water and find no hardship from not doing so, but this is a personal matter! From experience I find the more I drink the more I want and sweat. You should always carry some extra food such as Kendal Mint Cake, for emergencies.*

RUCKSACKS - *for day walking I use a climbing rucksack of about 40 litre capacity and although it leaves excess space it does mean that the sac is well padded, with an internal frame and padded shoulder straps. Inside apart from the basics for one day I carry gloves, balaclava, spare pullover and a pair of socks.*

MAP & COMPASS - *when I am walking I always have the relevant map - preferably 1:25,000 scale - open in my hand. This enables me to constantly check that I am walking the right way. In case of bad weather I carry a compass, which once mastered gives you complete confidence in thick cloud or mist.*

WALK RECORD CHART

Date Walked

Chew Reservoir - 12 miles ....

Crowden and Black Hill - 10 miles ....

Old Glossop and Torside - 13 miles ....

Thurlstone Moors - 10 miles ....

Cut Gate - 12 miles *8-9-90*

Howden Moor - 10 miles .... *4½ hrs*

Alport Castles - 9 miles *18/8/90*

Lose Hill - 8 miles .... *4 HRS (BLISTER)*

Chinley Churn - 8 miles ....

Kinder Downfall - 10 miles *11-8-90 4hrs*

Barber Booth Horseshoe - 10 miles . *6-7-91 4hrs 40min*

Crook Hill - 12 miles .... *1-9-90 4½ HRS*

The Hope Valley - 7 miles ....

Marsden to Edale - 25 miles ....

Kinder Circuit—High Level Route
 - 18 miles ....

Kinder Circuit—Low Level Route
 - 24 miles..

The Derwent Watershed Walk
 - 40 miles ....

THE JOHN MERRILL WALK BADGE

Complete six of the walks in this book and get the above special walk badge. Badges are a black cloth with walking man embroidered in four colours and measure - 3 1/2" in diameter.

BADGE ORDER FORM

Date and details of walks completed ....

....

NAME ....

ADDRESS ....

....
Price: £2.00 each including postage, VAT and signed completion certificate. Amount enclosed (Payable to JNM Publications) ....
From: JNM PUBLICATIONS, Winster, Matlock,
Derbyshire. DE4 2DQ.

℘ Winster (062988) 454 - 24hr answering service.
FAX: Winster (062988) 416

************ YOU MAY PHOTOCOPY THIS FORM *************

"I'VE DONE A JOHN MERRILL WALK" T SHIRT - Emerald Green with white lettering and walking man logo. Send £5.50 to JNM Publications stating size required.

OTHER BOOKS by JOHN N. MERRILL PUBLISHED by JNM PUBLICATIONS

CIRCULAR WALK GUIDES -
SHORT CIRCULAR WALKS IN THE PEAK DISTRICT
LONG CIRCULAR WALKS IN THE PEAK DISTRICT
CIRCULAR WALKS IN WESTERN PEAKLAND
SHORT CIRCULAR WALKS IN THE STAFFORDSHIRE MOORLANDS
SHORT CIRCULAR WALKS AROUND THE TOWNS & VILLAGES OF
THE PEAK DISTRICT
SHORT CIRCULAR WALKS AROUND MATLOCK
SHORT CIRCULAR WALKS IN THE DUKERIES
SHORT CIRCULAR WALKS IN SOUTH YORKSHIRE
SHORT CIRCULAR WALKS IN SOUTH DERBYSHIRE
SHORT CIRCULAR WALKS AROUND BUXTON
SHORT CIRCULAR WALKS IN THE HOPE VALLEY
40 SHORT CIRCULAR WALKS IN THE PEAK DISTRICT
CIRCULAR WALKS ON KINDER & BLEAKLOW
SHORT CIRCULAR WALKS IN SOUTH NOTTINGHAMSHIRE
SHIRT CIRCULAR WALKS IN CHESHIRE

CANAL WALKS -
VOL 1 - DERBYSHIRE & NOTTINGHAMSHIRE
VOL 2 - CHESHIRE & STAFFORDSHIRE
VOL 3 - STAFFORDSHIRE
VOL 4 - THE CHESHIRE RING
VOL 5 - LINCOLNSHIRE & NOTTINGHAMSHIRE
VOL 6 - SOUTH YORKSHIRE
VOL 7 - THE TRENT & MERSEY CANAL

JOHN MERRILL DAY CHALLENGE WALKS -
WHITE PEAK CHALLENGE WALK
DARK PEAK CHALLENGE WALK
PEAK DISTRICT END TO END WALKS
STAFFORDSHIRE MOORLANDS CHALLENGE WALK
THE LITTLE JOHN CHALLENGE WALK
YORKSHIRE DALES CHALLENGE WALK
NORTH YORKSHIRE MOORS CHALLENGE WALK
LAKELAND CHALLENGE WALK

INSTRUCTION & RECORD -
HIKE TO BE FIT.....STROLLING WITH JOHN
THE JOHN MERRILL WALK RECORD BOOK

MULTIPLE DAY WALKS -
THE RIVERS'S WAY
PEAK DISTRICT: HIGH LEVEL ROUTE
PEAK DISTRICT MARATHONS
THE LIMEY WAY
THE PEAKLAND WAY

COAST WALKS & NATIONAL TRAILS -
ISLE OF WIGHT COAST PATH
PEMBROKESHIRE COAST PATH
THE CLEVELAND WAY

PEAK DISTRICT HISTORICAL GUIDES -
DERBYSHIRE INNS - an A to Z guide
HALLS AND CASTLES OF THE PEAK DISTRICT & DERBYSHIRE
TOURING THE PEAK DISTRICT & DERBYSHIRE BY CAR
DERBYSHIRE FOLKLORE
PUNISHMENT IN DERBYSHIRE
CUSTOMS OF THE PEAK DISTRICT & DERBYSHIRE
WINSTER - a souvenir guide
ARKWRIGHT OF CROMFORD
TALES FROM THE MINES by Geoffrey Carr
PEAK DISTRICT PLACE NAMES by Martin Spray

JOHN MERRILL'S MAJOR WALKS -
TURN RIGHT AT LAND'S END
WITH MUSTARD ON MY BACK
TURN RIGHT AT DEATH VALLEY
EMERALD COAST WALK

COLOUR GUIDES -
THE PEAK DISTRICT.........Something to remember her by.

SKETCH BOOKS -
NORTH STAFFORDSHIRE SKETCHBOOK by John Creber

IN PREPARATION -
LONG CIRCULAR WALKS IN STAFFORDSHIRE
SHORT CIRCULAR WALKS IN WEST YORKSHIRE
SHORT CIRCULAR WALKS IN THE YORKSHIRE DALES
SHORT CIRCULAR WALKS IN THE LAKE DISTRICT
SHORT CIRCULAR WALKS IN NORTH YORKSHIRE MOORS
RUTLAND WATER CHALLENGE WALK
SNOWDONIA CHALLENGE WALK
FOOTPATHS OF THE WORLD - Vol 1 - NORTH AMERICA
HIKING IN NEW MEXICO

☞ Full list from JNM PUBLICATIONS, Winster, Matlock, Derbys.